DUBRC
TRAVEL GUIDE 2024

Explore The Enchanting Charms of Croatia's Pearl of The Adriatic

Rita R. Nowlin

Table Of Content

CHAPTER 1: AN OVERVIEW OF DUBROVNIK

Introduction

Stepping into Dubrovnik's cobblestone streets felt like entering a live time capsule. The historic city, set on the sun-drenched Adriatic Sea coastline, greeted me with its centuries-old charm and rich history. I marvelled at the spectacular sights of the dazzling blue seas that spread as far as the eye could reach as I wandered past the formidable city walls.

My vacation began with a stroll down the Stradun, the major street that cuts across the ancient town. This limestone-paved boulevard radiated elegance and antiquity, lined with lovely cafes, boutique stores, and exquisite facades. The echoes of previous footsteps echoed with each step, telling me that Dubrovnik had witnessed numerous stories throughout the centuries.

I couldn't resist the draw of Dubrovnik's ancient landmarks, such as the magnificent Fort Lovrijenac, which offered panoramic views of the city and sea. I found hidden jewels like Onofrio's Fountain and the mesmerising Rector's Palace as I explored the tight lanes and hidden courtyards.

However, it was the city's kind and inviting residents that actually made an effect on me. Whether I was eating delicious seafood in a cosy pub or telling stories with locals on the city walls, the people of Dubrovnik made me feel like a valued member of their society.

My trip to Dubrovnik was only getting started, but I knew it would leave an unforgettable impact on my heart, dragging me deeper into its intriguing history and timeless beauty.

Brief History Of Dubrovnik

Dubrovnik, known as the "Pearl of the Adriatic," has a rich and legendary past that has left an everlasting imprint on this stunning coastal city. Dubrovnik's history extends back to the 7th century, when it was founded as the Byzantine town of Ragusa on Croatia's Dalmatian coast. It grew into a strong maritime republic known as the Republic of Ragusa throughout the ages, and it became a significant role in Mediterranean trade.

Dubrovnik's richness during the Middle Ages was obvious in its spectacular architecture, which still survives today. The magnificent city walls that enclose the ancient town were built in the 13th century to protect it from attackers. These fortifications, together with ancient churches, monasteries, and palaces, have gained Dubrovnik World Heritage title from UNESCO.

The city experienced attacks from the Ottoman Empire and the Venetian Republic in the 16th century, but managed to preserve its freedom.

However, it was acquired by the French Empire in the early nineteenth century and ultimately became part of the Austro-Hungarian Empire. Following World War I, Dubrovnik became a part of the Kingdom of Yugoslavia, and then of modern-day Croatia.

Geography And Climate Condition

This mediaeval city on Croatia's southern coast is set between the Adriatic Sea's crystal-clear waves and the steep Dinaric Alps, providing a beautiful contrast between the turquoise sea and the dramatic, rocky environment.

The location of the city contributes significantly to its allure. The UNESCO World Heritage-listed Old Town is enclosed by solid mediaeval walls that overlook the sea, affording spectacular panoramic views of the coastline and adjacent islands. Lapad Bay, Dubrovnik's natural harbour, is a centre for nautical operations and a gateway to the Elaphiti Islands.

Dubrovnik has a Mediterranean climate, which is characterised by hot, dry summers and warm, rainy winters. Summers are the busiest season for tourists, with temperatures frequently reaching the mid-30s°C (mid-90s°F), making it ideal for beachgoers and outdoor lovers. Milder weather in spring and early fall is great for visiting the city's ancient treasures and enjoying leisurely walks around the city walls.

CHAPTER 2: PLANNING YOUR TRIP

Best Time To Visit

The summer months of June through August are the most popular for individuals who love warm weather and active outdoor activities. Dubrovnik has lengthy sunny days with temperatures ranging from 25°C to 35°C (77°F to 95°F) throughout this time of year. Tourists flock to the city, where they may bathe in the Adriatic Sea, see ancient monuments, and attend cultural events. It is worth mentioning, however, that costs are higher and the streets might become congested.

Consider going during the shoulder seasons of spring (April to May) or fall (September to October) for a more calm and cost-effective experience. Temperatures are nice, ranging from 18°C to 25°C (64°F to 77°F). During these months, there will be less tourists, reduced rates, and a more relaxed environment, but you will still be able to experience the splendour of Dubrovnik.

Getting To Dubrovnik

Those looking for ease and quickness can consider flying into Dubrovnik Airport. International travellers can use the airport since it is well-connected to major European cities. Visitors may easily access the city centre via taxi, shuttle, or public transit upon arrival.

Driving to Dubrovnik, on the other hand, may be an incredible road trip. The coastal roads provide stunning views of the Adriatic Sea and charming villages along the route. The picturesque Dalmatian coast may also be explored, with stops at secret coves and ancient places.

Taking a boat or cruise ship to Dubrovnik is a good choice if you want a more relaxed approach. Cruising the Adriatic lets you to take in the scenery while landing in elegance at the city's ancient port.

Entry And Visa Requirements

The entry and visa requirements for visiting Dubrovnik differ by country. For visits of any duration, citizens of the European Union (EU) and the European Free Trade Association (EFTA) do not require a visa to enter Croatia. Many other nations' citizens, including those from the United States, Canada, Australia, and New Zealand, are also eligible for visa-free entry for stays of up to 90 days in a 180-day period.

You will need to apply for a visa before visiting Croatia if you are not a citizen of a visa-exempt country. Visa applications can be made at your home country's Croatian embassy or consulate.

In addition to a valid passport or visa, you may be needed to produce the following documents at the Dubrovnik port of entry:

- Evidence of onward travel, such as a plane ticket or bus ticket.
- Evidence of lodging, such as a hotel reservation or Airbnb confirmation.
- Evidence of enough financial means to sustain your stay in Croatia.

Please keep in mind that the conditions listed above are subject to change, so always verify with the Croatian embassy or consulate in your home country before travelling.

Money And Budgeting

- **Currency**: Croatia's currency is the Euro (EUR). Banks, post offices, and currency exchange bureaus are all places where you may exchange money. It is also possible to convert currencies at the airport, albeit the prices are not always as favourable.

- **Debit and credit cards**: In Dubrovnik, credit and debit cards are generally accepted. However, having extra cash on hand is usually a smart idea, especially for little purchases and gratuities.

- **Accommodation**: One of the most costly aspects of a vacation to Dubrovnik is lodging. If you're on a tight budget, try staying outside of the Old Town at a hostel or guesthouse. Self-catering flats are also available, which might be a fantastic alternative for families or groups of friends.

- **Food**: Eating out in Dubrovnik, particularly in the Old Town, may be pricey. There are, however, some methods to save money on food. One alternative is to prepare your own meals in your lodging. Another alternative is to eat outside the Old Town, where the costs are often lower. Eating at street food booths and markets might also help you save money.

- **Transportation**: Walking is the greatest method to get about Dubrovnik. The city is tiny, and most of the major attractions are within walking distance of one another. There is a bus system that runs around the city if you need to utilise public transit. You may also get a Dubrovnik Card, which provides unlimited public transit as well as free entrance to several of the city's attractions.

- **Activities**: In Dubrovnik, there are several free and low-cost activities. You may, for example, stroll around the city walls, visit the Franciscan Monastery, and stroll along the Stradun, the major thoroughfare in the Old Town. A variety of free walking excursions are also available.

Getting Around Dubrovnik

Walking is the best method to see Dubrovnik's Old Town, which is a UNESCO World Heritage Site known for its well-preserved mediaeval architecture. Stroll through the historic city walls, see the Dubrovnik Cathedral, and explore the charming lanes dotted with shops and cafés. Wear comfortable shoes because the city's mountainous landscape can be taxing on your feet.

Dubrovnik has an effective public bus system that connects the Old Town with numerous neighbourhoods and attractions for longer travels. Buses are clean, safe, and inexpensive, making them a good alternative for travelling outside of the city centre. Taxis are also widely accessible, but they might be costly.

Consider taking a boat excursion if you want to discover the coastline in a new way. The Adriatic Sea position of Dubrovnik gives it a perfect starting point for trips to surrounding islands and secret coves.

Travel Tips & Packing

- **Travel Documents**: Make sure your passport is current, and find out whether you need a visa to visit Croatia. Maintain physical and digital copies of crucial papers such as your itinerary, travel insurance, and hotel bookings.

- **Lightweight, breathable clothes** is recommended for the warm Mediterranean environment. Remember to bring your swimwear, good walking shoes, and a light jacket for the chilly evenings.

- **Sun Protection**: To protect yourself from the sun, pack sunscreen, sunglasses, and a wide-brimmed hat.

- **Power Adapters**: Croatia utilises European Type C and Type F electrical outlets, so carry the appropriate adapters for your gadgets.

- **drugs**: Make sure you have adequate prescription drugs for your vacation and keep them in their original containers.

- **Language**: While English is widely spoken in Dubrovnik, learning a few basic Croatian words can be useful and appreciated by the locals.

- **The Croatian Kuna** is the official currency. It's a good idea to keep extra cash on hand for little transactions because credit cards aren't always accepted.

- **Comfortable Walking Shoes**: Exploring Dubrovnik on foot requires comfortable and durable footwear due to the city's cobblestone streets and steep climbs. Also Water shoes because Dubrovnik's beaches are primarily rocky, water shoes are a smart idea to protect your feet.

- **A travel guidebook** or a smartphone with a decent travel app may help you explore the city while also learning about its history and culture.

- **Staying hydrated** is critical, and Dubrovnik has several drinking fountains where you can replenish your bottle.

- **Mosquito repellent**: Mosquitoes may be a nuisance, especially in the nights, so bring some with you.

- **Rain Gear**: A light rain jacket or umbrella may come in helpful, as rains can occur even in the summer.

- **Power Bank**: Keep your gadgets charged while visiting the city, as you'll most likely be taking photographs and using navigation applications.

- **Reusable Shopping Bag:** Because Dubrovnik charges a plastic bag tax, bringing a reusable shopping bag can save you money while also reducing plastic waste.

CHAPTER 3:
TRANSPORTATION IN
DUBROVNIK

Public Bus

Bus tickets may be purchased at Libertas kiosks placed around the city or directly from the bus driver. Tickets purchased from the driver are significantly more expensive, therefore if feasible, acquire your tickets in advance.

A single bus ticket costs €1.73 and is good for 59 minutes after being stamped the first time. If you plan on taking the bus more than twice a day, a 24-hour bus pass at €5.31 may be worthwhile. The 24-hour pass entitles you to unlimited bus journeys for 24 hours after it is initially stamped.

Walking Tours

The Old Town Walking Tour is one of the most popular walking excursions. This trip visits all of the key Old Town attractions, including the Dubrovnik Cathedral, the Franciscan Monastery, and the Rector's Palace. You'll also learn about the city's intriguing history, which dates back to the 7th century and includes its role as a significant maritime force in the Middle Ages.

The Game of Thrones Walking Tour is another famous walking tour. This trip brings you to several of the popular TV show's filming locations, such as Lovrijenac Fortress (the Red Keep) and the Mineta Tower (the House of the Undying). You'll learn about the sequences that were shot at each site and hear show behind-the-scenes anecdotes.

There are also food walking tours offered if you are interested in eating. These trips will take you to some of Dubrovnik's top restaurants and cafés, where you can enjoy authentic Croatian food. You'll also learn about the culinary history and culture of the city.

Car Or Scooter Rental

- **Vehicle rental:** The average cost of hiring a car in Dubrovnik is between €50 and €75 per day. However, pricing might vary based on the parameters indicated above. hiring a car during peak season (June-August), for example, will be more expensive than hiring a car during off-season (September-May).

- **Rental of a scooter:** The average cost of hiring a scooter in Dubrovnik is between €25 and €45 per day. Prices will vary based on the model of scooter you hire, the duration of your rental, and the time of year.

Taxis And Ride-Sharing

- **Taxis**: Taxis are an easy method to move around Dubrovnik, particularly if you have luggage or are travelling in a group. Taxis may be found at the airport, train station, and throughout the city centre. You may also hail a cab on the street, although it is usually advisable to reserve one ahead of time, especially during high season.

  In Dubrovnik, the basic rate for a cab is about €3.50. The fee then rises in accordance with the distance travelled and the time of day. Taxi prices are controlled by the government, therefore there should be no pricing differences between taxi firms.

- **Ride-Sharing**: Uber and Bolt ride-sharing applications are also accessible in Dubrovnik. Ride-sharing is often less expensive than taxis, however finding a ride during high season might be more challenging.

on use a ride-sharing app, download the programme on your smartphone and set up an account. After creating an account, you may input your location and request a ride. The app will then connect you with a nearby driver.

The cost of a ride-sharing journey is determined on the distance travelled and the time of day. Uber and Bolt both have a minimum fare of roughly €2-3.

Information On Sightseeing Pass

In Dubrovnik, there are two primary sightseeing passes available:

- **The Dubrovnik Card** is a one-time fee that grants free entrance to several of the city's greatest sites, including the City Walls, the Rector's Palace, the Franciscan Monastery, and the Maritime Museum. It also provides savings on other activities including boat trips, cable car rides, and restaurants.
- **Dubrovnik Pass**: Similar to the Dubrovnik Card, the Dubrovnik Pass provides unlimited public transit and a complimentary boat journey to Lokrum Island.

Prices for the Dubrovnik Card and Dubrovnik Pass vary based on how long you buy them for.

CHAPTER 4: ACCOMMODATION SUGGESTIONS

Neighbourhoods In Dubrovnik

The Old Town is a labyrinth of small cobblestone lanes encircled by great stone walls that have safeguarded the city for centuries. Walking along the Stradun, the main street, you'll be surrounded by the elegance of well-preserved Baroque and Renaissance buildings, which are teeming with cafés, boutiques, and restaurants. The ancient centre of

Dubrovnik is a world unto itself, featuring buildings like as the Rector's Palace, Sponza Palace, and the renowned Dubrovnik Cathedral.

Ploe and Pile, two dynamic neighbourhoods to the north of the Old Town, are noted for their spectacular views of the city's red-tiled rooftops and the turquoise sea. Ploe is home to the majestic Fort Revelin, whereas Pile is home to the well-known Lovrijenac Fortress, which appears in the Game of Thrones series.

Lapad and Babin Kuk, located west of the Old Town, provide a more contemporary experience with gorgeous beaches, parks, and a wide range of lodgings. These areas are perfect for leisure and water activities, and they offer a unique perspective on Dubrovnik.

Resorts And Hotels

Luxury Hotels:

- **Dubrovnik Palace Hotel**: This 5-star hotel is perched on a rock overlooking the Old Town and the sea. It has opulent rooms and suites, a spa, many restaurants and bars, and a private beach. Prices begin about €500 per night.

- **Rixos Premium Dubrovnik**: This 5-star hotel is similarly perched on a cliff with views of the Old Town and the sea. It has opulent rooms and suites, a spa, many restaurants and bars, and a private beach. Prices begin around €400 per night.

- **The Hilton Imperial Dubrovnik** is a 5-star hotel in the centre of the Old Town. It has magnificent rooms and suites, a spa, many restaurants and bars, and breathtaking views of the city and the sea. Prices begin around €300 per night.

Mid-Range hotel:

- **Hotel Lapad**: This four-star hotel is in the Lapad neighbourhood, just a short bus ride from Old Town. It has luxurious rooms and suites, a spa, many restaurants and cafes, and an outdoor pool with views of the sea. Prices begin around €150 per night.

- **Hotel Neptun**: This four-star hotel is on the seafront, just a short walk from Old Town. It has pleasant rooms and suites, as well as a restaurant with views of the sea and an outdoor pool. Prices begin about €120 per night.

- **Hotel Adria**: This four-star hotel is in the Gruz neighbourhood, just a short bus ride from the Old Town. It has nice rooms and suites, as well as a restaurant and an outdoor pool. Prices begin about €100 per night.

Hotels on a budget:

- **City Hotel Dubrovnik**: Located in the Old Town, this 3-star hotel is a short walk from all of the main attractions. It has nice rooms and suites, as well as a breakfast area and a bar. Prices begin around €70 per night.

- **The Berkeley Hotel & Spa** is a 3-star hotel in the Lapad neighbourhood, a short bus ride from Old Town. It has nice rooms and suites, as well as a spa and a breakfast area. Prices begin around €60 per night.

- **Hostel One Dubrovnik**: Located in the Old Town, this hostel is a short walk from all of the main attractions. It has dorm beds and individual rooms, as well as a communal kitchen and a common lounge. Prices begin at €20 per night.

Guesthouses And Hostels

Guesthouses

- **Guest House Maria**: nestled in a calm neighbourhood within a short walk from the Old Town, this guesthouse is nestled in a quiet neighbourhood. There are several accommodation kinds available, including doubles, twins, and triples. A double room starts at roughly $60 per night.

- **Anchi Guesthouse & Bag Storage**: Located in the Old Town, this guesthouse is near to all of the important attractions. It has a range of accommodation types available, including singles, doubles, twins, and triples. A double room starts at roughly $70 per night.

- **Villa Orsula**: A 10-minute bus ride from the Old Town, this guesthouse is located on the Lapad Peninsula. It has a range of accommodation types available, including singles, doubles, twins, and triples. A double room starts at roughly $80 per night.

Hostels

- **Hostel Lina**: This hostel is in the Old Town, near to many of the important attractions. It provides a range of lodging alternatives, from shared dormitories to private rooms. Prices for a bed in a dorm room start about $20 per night.
- **Hostel Angelina Old Town Dubrovnik**: This hostel is in the Old Town, near all of the important attractions. It provides a range of lodging alternatives, from

shared dormitories to private rooms. Prices for a bed in a dorm room start about $25 per night.

- **Hostel More**: This hostel is on the Lapad Peninsula, about a 10-minute bus ride from the Old Town. It provides a range of lodging alternatives, from shared dormitories to private rooms. Prices for a bed in a dorm room start about $20 per night.

Vacation Rentals And Airbnb

- **Apartment Primavera**: Located in the centre of Dubrovnik, this one-bedroom apartment is within walking distance of all major attractions. It offers a spectacular view of the Old Town and the Adriatic Sea. The cost each night is $284.

- **Amazing Brand New 3 Bedroom villa & Pool House**: Located on a hilltop overlooking Dubrovnik, this luxury property is situated. It comes with three bedrooms, three bathrooms, a private pool, and a large patio with breathtaking views. The cost each night is $531.

- **Isabela Infinity House** is a contemporary mansion located in Vela Luka, about 30 minutes from Dubrovnik. It offers two bedrooms, two baths, a private beach, and an infinity pool. The cost each night is $167.

- **Seaside apartment with a lovely view**: This one-bedroom apartment is located in Jelsa, approximately 45 minutes from Dubrovnik. It features a private terrace with wonderful Adriatic Sea views. The cost each night is $95 per person.

- **Charming hacienda with private beachfront**: is located in the town of

Brijesta, about an hour from Dubrovnik. It features its own beach, a pool, and a spacious garden. The cost each night is $132.

Camping Possibilities

- **Camping Soline:** This campground is located just outside of Old Town, within walking distance of the beach. It has a range of camping choices, including spots for tents, caravans, and RVs. A tent spot costs roughly €20 per night.

- **Camping Auto-Camp**: This campsite is located on the Babin Kuk peninsula, approximately 6 km from the Old Town. It has a swimming pool, a children's playground, and a restaurant, as well as a range of camping alternatives. A tent spot starts at roughly €25 per night.

- **Camping Monika** is located on the Lapad peninsula, approximately 4 km from the Old Town. It has a swimming pool, a children's playground, and a restaurant, as well as a range of camping alternatives. A tent spot starts at roughly €20 per night.

- **Camping Odysseus**: This campground is located on the Babin Kuk peninsula, approximately 6 km from the Old Town. It has a swimming pool, a children's playground, and a restaurant, as well as a range of camping alternatives. A tent spot starts at roughly €25 per night.

CHAPTER 5: EXPLORING DUBROVNIK

Old Town Of Dubrovnik

City Walls:

These well-preserved 9th-century walls provide a unique perspective of Dubrovnik's stunning red-tiled roofs and the crystal-clear Adriatic Sea beyond.

The panoramic views from the walls are truly incredible. You'll be captivated by the magnificent Old Town, with its maze of small alleyways, old buildings, and vivid orange trees.

As you proceed down the path, the massive Minceta Tower, Lovrijenac Fortress, and other fortifications display their majestic presence. The walls also serve as a reminder of Dubrovnik's tenacity over the years, having endured countless battles.

Placa (Stradun):

From Pile Gate to Ploce Gate, this limestone-paved pedestrian thoroughfare serves as the city's heart and spirit. Stradun, which is lined with attractive cafés, boutique stores, and ancient sites, provides a fascinating voyage through time and culture.

You'll be charmed as you walk along its smooth cobblestones by the gorgeous architecture that surrounds you, displaying a harmonious combination of Gothic, Renaissance, and Baroque styles. The Onofrio Fountain is a spectacular greeting landmark, while the Franciscan Monastery and Sponza Palace are just a few of the architectural treasures to see.

Stradun's lively ambiance is great for sampling local delights such as candied orange peels and gelato, as well as sipping a cup of strong Croatian coffee. Stradun comes alive in the evening with vivid street acts, creating a beautiful environment not to be missed.

Historic Sites and Museums:

The city walls, provide an excellent vantage point from which to observe the city's distinct architectural combination of Gothic, Renaissance, and Baroque styles.

The Dubrovnik Old Town transports you to the Middle Ages, with tiny cobblestone lanes leading to attractive squares and old structures. The Rector's Palace and the Dubrovnik Cathedral are must-see attractions, displaying centuries of art and artefacts.

Museums like as the Dubrovnik Museum and the War Photo Limited give greater insights into the history and culture of Dubrovnik. You'll develop a great respect for Dubrovnik's legacy as you tour these locations, making your vacation an unforgettable and instructive experience.

The Islands Of Dubrovnik

Lokrum Island

It's only a short boat journey away. This little, wooded treasure in the Adriatic's crystal-clear waters has a rich history and a lovely environment. The island, which was formerly the private retreat of Benedictine monks, is now a wildlife reserve featuring beautiful gardens, rocky beaches, and diverse plant life.

On Lokrum, visitors may stroll through old olive trees, admire the stunning botanical garden, and come across friendly peacocks wandering freely. Don't pass up the chance to see the enigmatic Dead Sea, a little saltwater lake in the centre of the island. There is also a mediaeval stronghold and a mysterious monastery on the island.

Elafiti Islands

This archipelago, just a short boat trip from the historic walled city, consists of numerous islands, the most accessible and popular of which are Koloep, Lopud, and ipan. These tranquil isles provide a welcome respite from Dubrovnik's busy streets.

Koloep, the smallest of the three, is known for its lush woods and crystal-clear waters, making it ideal for nature lovers and swimmers. Lopud, often known as the "Island of Sun," is famous for its sandy beaches, picturesque settlements, and the ancient Sunj Beach. Meanwhile, the biggest, ipan, features vineyards, olive orchards, and stunning Renaissance architecture

Exploring the Elafiti Islands entails strolling through picturesque villages, hiking coastal pathways with stunning views, and dining on delicious seafood in rustic island eateries.

Island Of Mljet

Mljet is a tranquil refuge of natural beauty and cultural legacy, just a short boat ride from Dubrovnik.

Mljet is famous for its two linked saltwater lakes, Malo and Veliko Jezero, which are tucked inside a magnificent national park. A leisurely walk or bike ride around these lakes' picturesque pathways exposes lush woodlands, colourful meadows and rich animals. Don't pass up the opportunity to hire a kayak or small boat and visit St. Mary's Island, which is home to a 12th-century Benedictine abbey.

Mljet has an old history as well, with historical buildings like as the Roman palace and St. Mary's Church providing a look into the island's rich history.

Dubrovnik Day Trips

Ston and the Peljesac Peninsula

Your adventure will begin in the old city of Dubrovnik and will take you down the craggy coastline and through picturesque towns.

Ston, your first stop, is known for its spectacular defensive walls, which are commonly referred to as the "European Wall of

China." These 14th-century walls span over more than five km and provide insight into the region's historical significance. While at Ston, try the local specialties: fresh oysters and mussels grown in the neighbouring salt pans, a centuries-old tradition.

Continuing your journey, you'll pass through the tiny Peljesac Peninsula, an area known for its world-class wineries. Visit a local winery and sample the powerful red wines that are typical of this region.

The Peljesac Peninsula also has stunning views of the Adriatic Sea, making it a great area to unwind and enjoy nature. Dip your toes in the crystal-clear waters at one of the numerous isolated beaches, or visit the quaint town of Orebic for a taste of local cuisine and culture.

You'll return to Dubrovnik with a heart full of memories as the day comes to a close.

Cavtat

Cavtat, located just 18 km south of Dubrovnik, board a boat or drive along the gorgeous coastline route to Cavtat.

Cavtat, a picturesque seaside town with a rich history, has a lovely harbour, crystal-clear waters, and a laid-back environment. Spend the day exploring the small alleyways of the old town, visiting historic churches, and relaxing on the seaside promenade packed with cafés and restaurants. Don't miss the Rector's Palace, the Racic Mausoleum, and the tranquil Rai Family Mausoleum, all of which are located among beautiful cypress trees.

The beaches and coves of Cavtat are ideal for a refreshing dip, and water sports lovers may participate in activities such as snorkelling or kayaking. The stunning vistas from the hills surrounding Cavtat provide for fantastic photo opportunity. As the day comes to a close, savour some fresh seafood dishes at a local restaurant while taking in the quiet atmosphere of the town.

Montenegro

Your journey begins with a magnificent drive down the Adriatic coast, which provides spectacular views of the turquoise water, steep cliffs, and attractive coastal villages.

The magnificent Bay of Kotor, famed for its natural beauty and old architecture, is the first destination on your Montenegro day trip. Discover the picturesque squares, churches, and small cobblestone lanes of Kotor, which is surrounded by towering city walls and high cliffs.

Next, explore the coastal village of Perast, where you can see the famed Our Lady of the Rocks islet and eat local seafood at a beach café. Montenegro's varied landscapes provide chances for outdoor enthusiasts, ranging from trekking in the Loven National Park to bathing in the Adriatic's crystal-clear waters.

Return to Dubrovnik as the sun sets, having gained a better understanding for Montenegrin culture and its awe-inspiring natural beauty.

CHAPTER 6: DINING AND DRINKING IN DUBROVNIK

Croatian Traditional Dishes

- **Peka**: This meal highlights the region's slow-cooking culture. A combination of meats, generally veal or octopus, and seasonal vegetables is cooked to perfection under a bell-shaped dome. The finished product is a soft, delicious work of art.

- **Black Risotto**: Made with cuttlefish or squid ink, this dish not only tantalises the taste with its distinct saline flavour but also captivates with its beautiful ebony colour.

- **seafood Platter**: As a coastline city, Dubrovnik has a plentiful supply of fresh fish. Indulge in a seafood platter that includes grilled prawns, mussels, calamari, and a variety of fish.

- **Brodet**: Brodet is a delightful fish stew that mixes a variety of fish, garlic, and tomatoes and is cooked to a rich, hearty consistency.

- **Ston Oysters**: The village of Ston is famous for its exquisite oysters, which may be eaten fresh shucked with a splash of lemon or cooked in a variety of delectable ways.

- **Pata na brodu, or shellfish pasta**, is a popular Croatian dish. The meal is created with a tomato-based sauce with a variety of shellfish, including mussels, clams and prawns. Long noodles, such as spaghetti or linguine, are often used to make the pasta.

Seafood Delights

The local seafood scene is a tribute to freshness and simplicity. Dubrovnik's seafood pleasures are a sensory experience, from the lovely beachfront eateries to the lively open-air markets. Grilled Adriatic fish, such as sea bream and sea bass, are served simply with olive oil, garlic, and a sprinkle of Mediterranean herbs, allowing the natural flavours to show. For a more rustic flavour, consider black risotto, a dish cooked with cuttlefish ink, which gives it a distinct dark colour and a deep, saline flavour.

Another local specialty is oysters, which are collected in neighbouring Ston and are known for their sweet and briny flavour. Combine them with a glass of fresh local white wine for a seafood match made in heaven.

Cafes And Restaurants

Restaurants

- **Nautika Restaurant:** This fine-dining establishment on the riverfront offers breathtaking views of the Old Town. It provides fresh, local ingredients in a range of Mediterranean meals.

- **Proto Fish Restaurant**: Proto Fish Restaurant is a seafood restaurant in Old Town. It provides fresh seafood meals as well as traditional Croatian fare.

- **Lokanda Pescaria** is a family-run restaurant in the Old Town. It provides traditional Croatian cuisine prepared with fresh, seasonal ingredients.

If you're on a tight budget, there are plenty of cheap cafés and eateries in Dubrovnik. Here are a few suggestions:

- **Amici Cafe** - Bistro: Located in the Old Town, this cafe-bistro serves Italian cuisine. It offers a wide range of coffee beverages, pastries, and sandwiches.

- **Veseljak pizza**: This is located in the Old Town. It offers a selection of pizzas as well as other Italian cuisine.
- **Lokanda Konoba**: This historic Croatian pub is located in the Old Town. It delivers authentic Croatian cuisine at moderate costs.

Vegetarian And Vegan Alternatives

In Dubrovnik, vegetarian alternatives include "Punjene Paprike" (stuffed bell peppers) loaded with a delightful mixture of rice and vegetables, or "Blitva s Krumpirom" (Swiss chard with potatoes), a simple yet flavorful side dish. Many eateries also serve "Palenta," a cornmeal-based dish that is frequently topped with mushrooms or spinach.

Vegans will be pleased with the local options as well. "Pasta Primavera" with fresh tomatoes, basil and olive oil, or "Soparnik," a savoury pastry packed with Swiss chard, garlic and olive oil, are also recommended. Vegan pastries and sweets, such as fruit sorbets or nut-based cakes, are frequently available in Dubrovnik's lovely cafés.

Furthermore, the city's numerous farmers' markets offer a variety of fresh fruits and vegetables, allowing you to prepare your own plant-based meals at your lodging.

Local Wines And Beverages

The wine culture of Dubrovnik has a long and illustrious history, reaching back to Roman times. The city's distinct environment, with abundance of sunshine and mild sea breezes, creates ideal circumstances for vineyards to thrive, producing some remarkable wines.

Plavac Mali, a red wine created from the indigenous grape of the same name, is one of the most well-known local types. It's a must-try for every wine aficionado, thanks to its powerful and fruity flavour. The Plavac Mali grapes in the Dinga and Postup areas, just a short drive from Dubrovnik, are particularly well-known.

Aside from wine, Dubrovnik has a wide selection of pleasant beverages. Rakija, a traditional fruit brandy, is a popular option that comes in a variety of flavours such as grape, plum, and fig. Limunada, a tangy lemonade that is ideal for the warm Mediterranean environment, is also available.

CHAPTER 7:SHOPPING IN DUBROVNIK

Souvenirs And Handcrafted Items

Here are some suggestions for souvenirs and handcrafted goods to purchase while in Dubrovnik:

- **Handmade lace**: Dubrovnik is famous for its gorgeous handmade lace, which is created using ancient skills passed down through generations. Many souvenir stores across the city sell handcrafted lace goods such as tablecloths, napkins, doilies, and jewellery.

- **Olive oil:** Dubrovnik, like the rest of Croatia, is a significant producer of olive oil. Many souvenir stores and marketplaces sell high-quality olive oil prepared from local olives. Try some of the numerous types of olive oil available, such as Istrian olive oil and Korula olive oil.

- **Wine**: Croatia is a wine-producing country, and Dubrovnik has a wide selection of local wines to pick from. Red wine, white wine, and rosé wine made from native grape varietals such as Plavac Mali and Poip are available. Try some of the local wines to select the right one to bring back with you.

- **Lavender products**: Another popular commodity in Croatia is lavender, which can be found in souvenir stores in the form of lavender soap, lavender oil, and lavender sachets.

- **Handcrafted jewellery**: There are many creative jewellery manufacturers in Dubrovnik who produce magnificent pieces from a range of materials, including gold, silver, and gemstones.

Handcrafted jewellery may be found in various souvenir stores and marketplaces across the city.

- **Traditional Croatian clothes**: For a one-of-a-kind keepsake, try purchasing a piece of traditional Croatian attire. Many souvenir stores and marketplaces sell traditional Croatian attire such as dresses, shirts, and ties.

Markets And Shops

Markets

One of the greatest locations to learn about local culture and buy fresh fruit is at one of Dubrovnik's numerous markets. Gru Market and Gunduliceva Poljana Market are the two major marketplaces.

- **Gru Market** is located near the ferry terminal and is open daily except Sunday. It's an excellent source of fresh fruits and vegetables, fish, meat, and dairy products. Souvenirs and other local crafts are also available.

- **Gunduliceva Poljana Market** is open every day and is located in the Old Town. Although it is smaller than Gru Market, it is nevertheless an excellent destination to get fresh food and gifts. It's also an excellent spot to sample some local cuisine, such as fritule (fried dough balls) and prut (Dalmatian prosciutto).

Dubrovnik also has other markets like: **Ploe Market**, A tiny market in the Old Town that is open every day. **Lapad Market**, A tiny market in the Lapad neighbourhood that is open every day and **Dubrovnik Farmers Market**, A weekly market hosted in the Old Town every Saturday.

Shops

Dubrovnik boasts a variety of boutiques and speciality stores for more expensive shopping. Stradun, the main street of the Old Town, is home to the primary shopping district. Everything from clothing and shoes to jewellery and souvenirs may be found here.

The following are some of the most popular stores on Stradun:

- **Boutique Croata:** A store that sells high-quality Croatian clothing.
- **Dubrovacka Kuca** is a store that sells traditional Croatian handicrafts and gifts.
- **Museum Shop**: A store that sells souvenirs and reproductions of artefacts from the museums in Dubrovnik.

Shopping Avenues

Shopping Centre Sr is the place to go if you want a one-stop shop for all of your shopping requirements. This enormous retail centre contains over 100 stores, including worldwide names such as Zara, H&M, and Mango. It also features a movie theatre, a bowling alley, and a number of restaurants and cafés.

Dubrovnik Shopping Mineta is another prominent shopping mall in Dubrovnik. Although this mall is smaller than Shopping

Centre Sr, it nevertheless boasts an excellent assortment of retailers, including international names and local boutiques. It also features a pizzeria, a casino with slot machines, and a beauty salon.

If you want a more traditional shopping experience, you should go to the Old Town. The Old Town is a UNESCO World Heritage Site with tiny streets and alleys packed with businesses. Everything from souvenirs and handicrafts to high-end clothes and jewellery is available.

Stradun is one of the most popular retail alleys in the Old Town. Stradun is the Old Town's principal pedestrian thoroughfare, dotted with shops and restaurants. Stradun sells everything from souvenirs and handicrafts to high-end clothes and jewellery.

Prijeko is another renowned retail street in the Old Town. Prijeko is a small street parallel to Stradun. It is lined with boutiques and smaller stores, as well as a few cafes and eateries.

If you're seeking for something out of the ordinary, you should go to the **Gru Market**. The Gru Market is a big outdoor market where you may purchase fresh vegetables, seafood, and other locally produced items. The market also sells souvenirs and handicrafts.

CHAPTER 8: ENTERTAINMENT AND NIGHTLIFE

Pubs And Bars

Here are a handful of Dubrovnik's most popular pubs and bars:

- **The Gaffe**: This traditional Irish bar is a favourite with both locals and visitors. It's a terrific spot to drink Guinness while listening to live Irish music.

- **Pub Dubrovnik:** Located in the centre of the Old Town, this pub serves a broad variety of beers on tap as well as drinks and nibbles. It's a favourite hangout for both visitors and residents, and it's a terrific area to people-watch and absorb up the Old Town ambiance.

- **Celtic Bar Belfast Dubrovnik**: Located in the Pile Gate neighbourhood of Dubrovnik, this bar serves a broad variety of beers on tap as well as drinks and nibbles. It's a popular place to watch sports and offers a live music stage.

- **Buzz Bar** is located on the Stradun, the main thoroughfare in Old Town. It's a popular hangout for drinks and people-watching.

- **Cave Bar More**: This one-of-a-kind bar is housed in a natural cave overlooking the sea. It's a fantastic spot for a drink and maybe live music while admiring the breathtaking surroundings.

Nightclubs

The following are the most popular Dubrovnik nightclubs:

- **Culture Club Revelin**: This nightclub is housed within a 16th-century fortress, giving it a distinct and evocative atmosphere. It's one of Dubrovnik's most popular nightclubs, and it plays a wide range of music, including house, techno, and pop.

- **Café & Night bar Level**: This nightclub is located in Old Town and is a wonderful choice if you want a more private environment. It mixes house, techno, and R&B music.

- **Club Lazareti**: Located just outside the Old Town, this nightclub is noted for its outdoor patio and excellent views of the city. It broadcasts a wide range of music, including house, techno, and hip hop.

Cultural Displays

The city's well-preserved mediaeval architecture is one of the city's most prominent cultural exhibitions. Visitors are taken back in time as they explore the historic city walls, cobblestone streets, and spectacular Gothic and Renaissance structures of the Old Town. The architecture of the city acts as a living museum, providing a look into its past and a feeling of the complex cultural fabric that distinguishes Dubrovnik.

Furthermore, Dubrovnik is well-known for its cultural heritage festivals and events. The Dubrovnik Summer Festival, staged in open-air locations against the backdrop of the city's historical attractions, is a highlight. These events highlight both local and foreign artists' artistic skills, promoting a greater respect for the city's cultural variety.

Another important component of Dubrovnik's cultural showcase is its gastronomy. Restaurants and marketplaces in the city serve exquisite Mediterranean fare such as fresh fish, olive oil, and local wines. Trying these culinary treats is a cultural experience in and of itself, reflecting the region's long-standing gastronomic traditions.

Festivals & Events

Spring

- Dubrovnik Carnival (February): This yearly event combines colourful costumes, vibrant parades and traditional music and dancing.

- Easter (April): Easter is observed with seriousness and excitement in Dubrovnik, a profoundly Catholic city. Throughout the city, there are special church services, processions, and concerts.

Summer

- Dubrovnik Summer Festival (July-August): This world-renowned festival includes classical music concerts, opera, ballet, and theatre acts. The event is held at a variety of locations across the city, including the Rector's Palace, the Franciscan Monastery, and Lokrum Island.
- Midsummer Scene (June-August): This event features outdoor performances of Shakespeare's plays. The concerts are held at the magnificent Fort Bokar, which has breathtaking views of the city and the Adriatic Sea.

Autumn

- Dubrovnik International Film Festival (October): This festival features independent and international films from throughout the world. The festival screenings are held in several theatres across the city, and additional activities such as panel discussions and Q&A sessions with directors are also held.

- Dubrovnik Good Food Festival (October) honours the region's rich culinary tradition. Visitors may taste excellent cuisine and beverages from local restaurants and suppliers, as well as participate in cooking demos and seminars.

Winter

- Christmas in Dubrovnik (December): During the Christmas season, the city is converted into a wintry paradise. Throughout the city, there are festive markets, ice skating rinks, and Christmas music.

- Dubrovnik New Year's Eve (December): Dubrovnik is a fantastic site to ring in the new year. The city has a festive atmosphere, with special events and festivities taking place in numerous locations.

CHAPTER 9: OUTDOOR RECREATION

Swimming And Beaches

 The Adriatic Sea's crystal-clear waters entice visitors to enjoy a relaxing dip or participate in a variety of water sports. Banje Beach, just outside the city walls, is a great place to cool down and take in the views of the Old Town. This pebbly beach is known for its lively ambiance, with parasols, sun loungers and a beach bar for visitors looking to soak up the rays in style.

Sveti Jakov Beach is a must-see for those looking for more quiet choices. This beach cove, nestled behind green cliffs, offers a calm escape with a spectacular view of Dubrovnik's skyline.

Nature Reserves And Hiking Trails

Natural enthusiasts will adore the natural reserves in and around Dubrovnik. A short boat trip away, the Lokrum Island Nature Reserve offers a unique getaway into a beautiful sanctuary complete with floral gardens, exotic peacocks, and calm walking trails. A little further out, Mljet National Park provides tourists with the opportunity to immerse themselves in untouched environment, where thick woods meet crystal-clear lakes.

The Dubrovnik area is a hiking enthusiast's dream. A popular option is the Sveti Jakov route, which gives stunning views of the Old Town and the Adriatic Sea. The Ston Walls walk follows the old walls and provides insight into the region's rich history. There are also various paths in the Konavle region that weave past vineyards, olive orchards, and lovely towns.

Exploring Dubrovnik's nature reserves and hiking paths is an excellent opportunity to experience the region's natural beauty while escaping the hustle and bustle of the city.

Water Activities

Sea kayaking is a popular activity that allows you to paddle around the historic city walls and explore secret caves and bays. You'll get a unique perspective of Dubrovnik's famed Old Town, with its red-tiled rooftops and centuries-old architecture, while you glide across the turquoise seas.

Sunbathing on Dubrovnik's lovely beaches is a must for anyone looking for a more relaxed experience. Banje Beach, for example, is a beautiful area where you can soak up the Mediterranean sun and cool down with a refreshing dip.

Consider snorkelling or scuba diving if you're feeling more daring. The clean waters of the Adriatic are home to a plethora of marine life, shipwrecks, and underwater caverns that demand investigation.

The lively harbour of Dubrovnik also acts as a launching point for boat cruises to adjacent islands like Lokrum and Elaphiti, providing a great chance for island hopping, swimming, and sampling local delicacies.

Filming Locations For Game Of Thrones

The city walls, which also served as the magnificent defences of King's Landing, are a must-see. Walking along these old walls offers tourists breathtaking panoramic views of the city and the Adriatic Sea, allowing them to recreate moments starring Cersei Lannister, Tyrion Lannister, and other well-known characters.

Lovrijenac Fortress, which stands magnificently on the brink of the sea, is another renowned location. It served as the Red Keep, the Iron Throne's seat of authority. While touring this massive facility, you may imagine important scenes in the series.

Finally, Cersei's walk of atonement took place on the Jesuit Staircase, a famous series of steps in the centre of the Old Town. It's a powerful setting for retracing her travels and appreciating the complexities of Game of Thrones narrative.

CHAPTER 10: ITINERARY SUGGESTIONS

Weekend Itinerary

Day 1: Explore Old Town

Begin your journey by exploring the centre of Dubrovnik, the Old Town. Stroll around the historic city walls, which provide spectacular views of the turquoise Adriatic Sea and red-tiled houses. Explore the city's principal boulevard, the Stradun, which is dotted with attractive boutiques and cafés.

Visit the old Rector's Palace, which houses the Dubrovnik Museum, as well as the imposing Sponza Palace. Enjoy some fresh seafood at a local restaurant in the evening while viewing the sunset.

Island hopping on Day 2

Take a boat journey to the adjacent Elaphiti Islands or the gorgeous Lokrum Island to see the natural beauty of Dubrovnik's surrounds. These lovely spots are ideal for swimming, hiking, and picnics in peaceful surroundings.

Return to Dubrovnik in the afternoon to see the Dominican Monastery and the Franciscan Monastery, which has one of Europe's oldest operating pharmacies.

Day 3: Relaxation and Culture

Begin your day with a trip to Mount Srd, which is accessible by cable car and offers panoramic views of the city. Then, visit the Dubrovnik Cathedral and the city's various churches and chapels to learn about the city's rich cultural legacy.

Finish your journey with a relaxed day at Banje Beach, where you may sip cocktails and swim in the crystal-clear seas. To round up your amazing Dubrovnik experience, dine on Croatian food at a local restaurant in the evening.

5 Days Itinerary

Day 1: Visit Dubrovnik's Old Town.

Begin your Dubrovnik vacation by exploring the Old Town's mediaeval beauty. Begin with the main entrance, Pile Gate, then walk along Stradun, the marble-paved main street. Visit the Rector's Palace, Sponza Palace, and the beautiful Dubrovnik Cathedral. Climb the mediaeval city walls for sweeping vistas of the terracotta roofs and the glistening Adriatic Sea.

Island hopping on Day 2

Set out on an island-hopping expedition. Take a boat to Lokrum Island, which is famed for its rich gardens and calm ambience. Discover the floral gardens as well as the mediaeval monastery. Head to the adjacent Elafiti Islands in the afternoon for beautiful beaches and crystal-clear seas. At a beachfront restaurant, sip local wine and savour fresh fish.

Day 3: Culinary Delights in Dubrovnik

Spend the day sampling delicious Croatian food. Begin your journey in Gruz Market, where you may sample fresh goods and mix with the locals. Enjoy a classic konoba fish feast. Then, enrol in a culinary class to learn how to make traditional Dalmatian delicacies like peka and black risotto.

Day 4: Day Trip to Montenegro

A day excursion to Montenegro takes you beyond Croatia's boundaries. Drive along the

UNESCO World Heritage-listed Bay of Kotor. Explore Kotor's lovely town, climb the city walls for stunning views, and visit Our Lady of the Rocks island. In the evening, return to Dubrovnik.

Day 5: Rest and Beach Time

Finish your trip to Dubrovnik with a day of rest. Sunbathe and swim in the Adriatic at Banje Beach, only a short walk from the Old Town. Spend a day at the spa or simply relax by the sea, savouring your last moments in this wonderful city.

7 Days Itinerary

Arrival on Day One

Arrive in Dubrovnik and check into your hotel. Take a walk around the famed Old Town walls for panoramic views, then dine at a local restaurant.

Day 2: Explore Old Town

Explore the labyrinthine lanes of the UNESCO-listed Old Town, appreciate the Rector's Palace, and pay a visit to the Sponza Palace. Take a cable car journey to Mount Srd at sunset for spectacular views.

Island hopping on Day 3

For beautiful beaches and lush scenery, take a boat cruise to the adjacent Elafiti Islands of Lopud, Sipan, and Kolocep. At a coastal restaurant, savour fresh seafood.

Day 4: Historical Observance

Explore ancient locations such as Fort Lovrijenac, the City Walls of Dubrovnik, and the Franciscan Monastery. Don't miss out on seeing the world-famous Dubrovnik Cathedral.

Day 5: The Cuisine of Dubrovnik

Take a culinary tour around the busy market and lunch in a traditional Konoba to sample local cuisine. Enjoy a night out while sampling Croatian wines.

Day 6: Outing

Day excursion to the picturesque village of Cavtat or the stunning Montenegrin seashore.

Day 7: Beach Time

Swim in the crystal-clear waters at Banje Beach and soak up the sun. Spend your final evening on the Adriatic Sea drinking beverages.

Family Friendly Itinerary

Day 1: Visit the Old Town

Begin your tour by experiencing Dubrovnik's famous Old Town. Stroll around the mediaeval city walls and stop by the picturesque squares of Lua and Gundulieva Poljana. Don't miss a stroll through the renowned Stradun, where you may sample excellent ice cream or traditional Croatian sweets.

Island hopping on Day 2
Take a day excursion to the adjacent Elafiti Islands with your family. Visit Koloep, Lopud, and Ipan to unwind on lovely beaches, swim in crystal-clear seas, and have a picnic with your loved ones.

Dubrovnik Cable Car on Day 3
Take an exciting cable car journey to the summit of Mount Srd for panoramic views of the city and the Adriatic Sea. Explore the Museum of the Homeland War as your children play on the playground.

Lokrum Island on Day 4
Lokrum Island, a short boat trip from Dubrovnik, has rich floral gardens, a mediaeval

monastery, and free-roaming peacocks. It's a naturalist's dream and a great site for family adventure.

Day 5: Sea Kayaking

Get a different view on Dubrovnik by embarking on a sea kayaking experience. Paddle through the city walls and secret coves for a fun and exciting day for all ages.

Dubrovnik Beaches on Day 6

Spend a day relaxing, swimming, and soaking up the Croatian sun at Banje or Lapad Beach.

CHAPTER 11: USEFUL INFORMATION

Emergency Phone Numbers

Here are some other emergency phone numbers that you may find handy while in Dubrovnik:

Police: 192

Traffic Police: +385 (20) 443 666

Maritime Police: +385 (20) 443 555

Road Assistance: 1987

Ambulance: 194

Fire Department: 193

Health Centre: +385 (20) 416 866

Search and Rescue at Sea: 195

Dubrovnik General Hospital: +385 (20) 431 777

It's a good idea to keep these phone numbers on your phone before travelling to Dubrovnik, so you'll have them handy if you need them. You can also write them down on paper and store them in your wallet or handbag.

If you are calling from a mobile phone, you may need to first enter the Croatian country code **(+385)**, followed by the emergency number.

If you are unsure which emergency number to dial, simply dial **112**. This is the general emergency number, and the operator will link you to the proper service.

Safety Recommendation

- **Keep an eye out for pickpockets**. Pickpockets are widespread in all tourist places, although they are most active in busy areas such as Dubrovnik's Old Town. Keep your valuables close to hand at all times and don't leave them unattended.

- **Be wary of con artists**. Tourists are targeted by a variety of frauds in Dubrovnik, including impersonating taxi drivers and tour companies. Before scheduling any excursions or transportation, do your homework and only use licenced providers.

- **When strolling on the cobblestone streets, use caution**. The streets of Dubrovnik are built of slick cobblestones, so be cautious when walking, especially if you're wearing sandals or heels.

- **Keep hydrated**. Dubrovnik can get quite hot in the summer, so staying hydrated by drinking plenty of water is essential. Sugary beverages, which might dehydrate you, should be avoided.

- **Put on sunblock and a hat**. In Dubrovnik, the sun may be quite intense, therefore wear sunscreen and a hat to protect yourself from the sun's damaging rays.

- **When swimming, use caution**. The Adriatic Sea has powerful currents in certain spots, therefore swim only in areas monitored by lifeguards.
- **Avoid going out at night by yourself**. Avoid wandering alone at night in Dubrovnik, particularly in less well-lit places. If you must go alone, keep an eye on your surroundings and remain in well-lit places.

Communication And Language

- **English is commonly understood**. The majority of Dubrovnik residents, particularly those employed in the tourism business, speak English. Visitors who make an effort to acquire a few simple Croatian words, on the other hand, are always welcomed.

- **Learn a few fundamental Croatian phrases**. This will demonstrate that you are appreciative of the local culture and language, and it may also assist you in everyday circumstances. Here are a few sentences to remember:

  Izvinite (excuse me)

  Dobar dan (good day)

  Molim (please)

  Hvala (thank you)

  Ne razumijem (I don't understand)

  Doviđenja (goodbye)

  Da (yes)

  Ne (no)

- **Be understanding and patient**. Even if you speak Croatian, you may have communication difficulties. This is due to the fact that Croatian is a Slavic language that may be unknown to

English speakers. Be patient and understanding, and do not be hesitant to seek assistance.

- **Use facial expressions and body language.** Body language and facial gestures may be extremely useful in communicating, especially when a language barrier exists. Make eye contact, smile, and utilise gestures to express your message.

- **Make no apologies about making blunders.** When learning a new language, everyone makes mistakes. The key thing is to keep trying to communicate. Don't be scared to make errors; the locals will appreciate your efforts.

- **Slowly and clearly speak.** This will allow the person you're conversing with to better comprehend you.

- **Slang and idioms should be avoided.** Even if a native speaker is fluent in English, these might be difficult to grasp.
- **Take note of cultural variations.** In Croatia, for example, interrupting someone while they are speaking is considered impolite.
- **Don't be hesitant to seek assistance.** If you're having trouble communicating, don't be hesitant to seek assistance from a local or hotel staff.

Internet Access And SIM Cards

- **Free Public Wi-Fi** is available for free: In Dubrovnik, many hotels, restaurants, and cafés provide free public Wi-Fi. This can be a simple method to connect to the internet, but keep in mind that public Wi-Fi networks can be sluggish and unsafe. Avoid utilising public Wi-Fi for important operations like banking or online shopping.

- **Prepaid SIM Cards:** A prepaid SIM card from a Croatian mobile company is another alternative. This will provide you with nationwide access to the internet and cellphone service. Prepaid SIM cards are reasonably priced and may be acquired at a variety of kiosks, post offices, and mobile phone retailers.

- **eSIM Cards:** You may also buy an eSIM card for Croatia if you have a suitable smartphone. eSIM cards are digital SIM cards that can be remotely activated. If you don't want to carry about an actual SIM card, this might be a practical choice.

The best approach to gain internet connection in Dubrovnik is determined by your specific requirements and preferences. If you're on a tight budget and don't want a lot of bandwidth, free public Wi-Fi may be a smart alternative. If you want more data or wish to access the internet while on the road, a prepaid SIM card or eSIM card is a better option.

Local And Customs Etiquette

- **When visiting churches and monasteries, dress modest**ly. While beachwear is permitted, it is best to cover yourself when strolling through the city.
- **Croatians are noted for their gracious hospitality.** When meeting new people, extend a handshake and make eye contact. A pleasant "Dobar dan" (good day) or "Hvala" (thank you) goes a long way.
- **Tipping is usual**, with restaurants often tipping between 10-15% of the bill.

Rounding up the tab is valued at cafés and bars.

- **Respect for Historic Sites**: When touring the Old Town, keep the historic significance in mind. Avoid touching or leaning against old walls, and keep loud conversations to a minimum near cultural landmarks.

- **Wait for the host to begin the meal** and then say "Dobar tek" before eating. Keep your hands but not your elbows on the table.

- **Beach Etiquette**: At the beach, wear proper swimwear. Sunbathing without a top is normally permitted, however naked sunbathing is not.

- **While many people understand English**, making an attempt to speak a few Croatian phrases is welcomed.

Insider Tips

- **Stay inside the city wall.** This is the most expensive option, but it is the finest way to experience the city's distinct vibe. The Old Town is a labyrinth of small streets and alleys dotted with stores, restaurants, and cafés. Many of Dubrovnik's most prominent sights, including as the Rector's Palace, the Franciscan Monastery, and the Onofrio's Fountain, are also located here.

- **Explore by foot.** Dubrovnik is a relatively walkable city, and exploring it on foot is the best way to experience it. Take your time exploring the Old Town and getting lost in the maze of streets. From lovely stores to cosy eateries, you'll find hidden jewels around every turn.

- **Take the city bus to get about**. Dubrovnik has an outstanding and reasonably priced public bus system. Tickets can be purchased from bus drivers or newsstands. Buses circulate around the city on a regular basis, and numerous routes connect the Old Town to the suburbs and adjacent beaches.

- **Consume fresh fish from the area**. Dubrovnik is famous for its fresh seafood, so eat some while you're there. Many wonderful restaurants in Old Town provide fresh seafood meals such grilled fish, seafood risotto, and black risotto.

- **Stay away from the masses**. If you're visiting Dubrovnik during the summer, go early in the morning or late in the afternoon to escape the crowds. During the shoulder seasons (May-June and September-October), the city is also significantly less busy.

- **Take a stroll along the city walls.** The views from the city walls of the Old Town and the Adriatic Sea are breathtaking. The full wall circuit may be completed in around two hours.

- **Pay a visit to the Rector's Palace.** The Rector's Palace, which was originally the residence of Dubrovnik's Rector, is today one of the city's most renowned tourist attractions. The palace houses a museum that covers the history of Dubrovnik.

- **Travel by boat to Lokrum Island.** Lokrum Island is a little island off the coast of Dubrovnik. It's a popular swimming, sunbathing, and trekking destination.

- **Try some of the native cuisine in Dubrovnik.** Dubrovnik's cuisine is distinct, influenced by its Mediterranean environment. Local specialties to try include black risotto, pata na brodu (shellfish pasta), and rozata (a custard dessert).

Eco-Friendly Travel Suggestions

- **Dubrovnik has an effective public transit system**, which includes buses and ferries. Choosing these means of transportation not only saves carbon emissions but also allows you to enjoy gorgeous vistas along the route.

- **Walking and cycling**: The Old Town of Dubrovnik is best explored on foot, and bicycles may be rented for eco-friendly excursions of the city and its surroundings. This allows you to enjoy the local culture, architecture, and landscape while reducing air pollution.

- **Choose eco-friendly accommodations** that prioritise energy efficiency and water conservation. Many Dubrovnik hotels and guesthouses have implemented environmentally friendly practises.

- **Support eco-friendly tour companies** who promote sustainable tourism, such as hiking, kayaking, and snorkelling trips that teach participants about local ecosystems and conservation initiatives.

- **Waste Reduction**: Reduce waste to protect the environment. Bring a reusable water bottle and shopping bag, and dispose of waste properly.

- **Local food:** Enjoy wonderful local food while supporting restaurants that employ locally produced and organic products, lowering your meal's carbon footprint.

Conclusion On Responsible Tourism

Respecting the city's sensitive nature, limiting your environmental imprint, and helping local communities are all part of responsible tourism in Dubrovnik. Visitors should prioritise cultural sensitivity, minimising their influence on historic monuments, and respecting local culture. Exploring sites outside of the Old Town that are less well-known can help lessen crowds.

Local governments should continue to put measures in place to regulate tourist numbers and manage cruise ship arrivals. They should also invest in long-term infrastructure, waste management, and the promotion of regional goods and customs.

The tourist business must use sustainable practises, such as providing eco-friendly lodging, responsible excursions, and assisting in the preservation of natural and cultural assets.

Maps

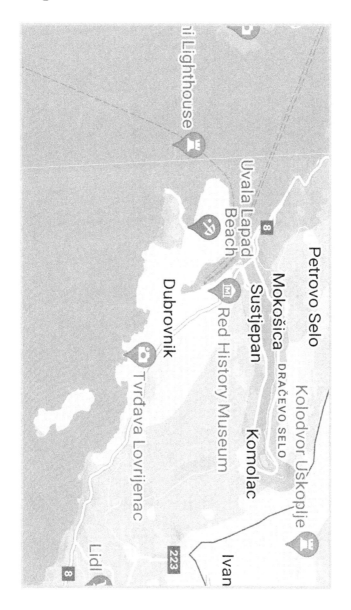

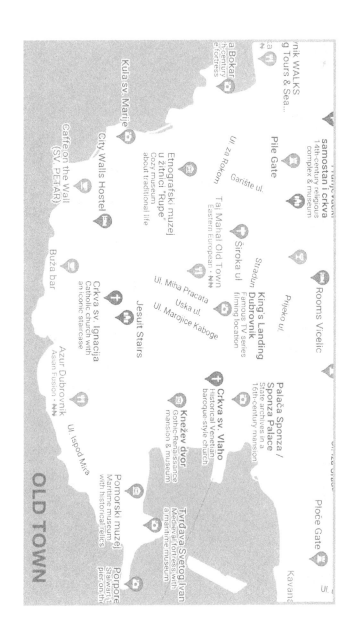

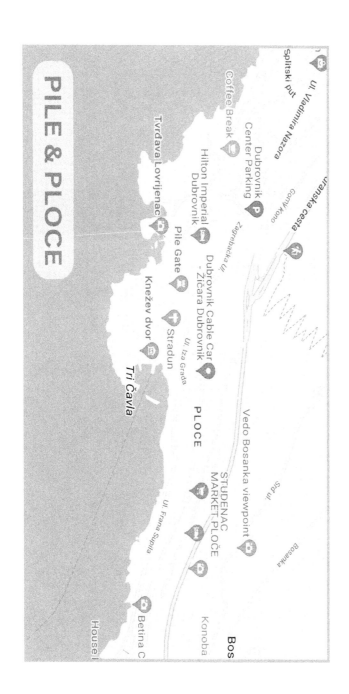

PILE & PLOCE

Splitski put

Ul. Vladimira Nazora

Coffee Break

uranska cesta

Dubrovnik
Center Parking

Gorn/ Kono

Zagrebačka ul.

Tvrđava Lovrijenac

Hilton Imperial
Dubrovnik

Pile Gate

Dubrovnik Cable Car
- Žičara Dubrovnik

Ul. Iza Grada

PLOCE

Vedo Bosanka viewpoint

Knežev dvor

Stradun

Tri Čavla

Srd ul.

STUDENAC
MARKET PLOČE

Bosanka

Ul. Frana Supila

Betina C

Konoba

Bos

House I

115

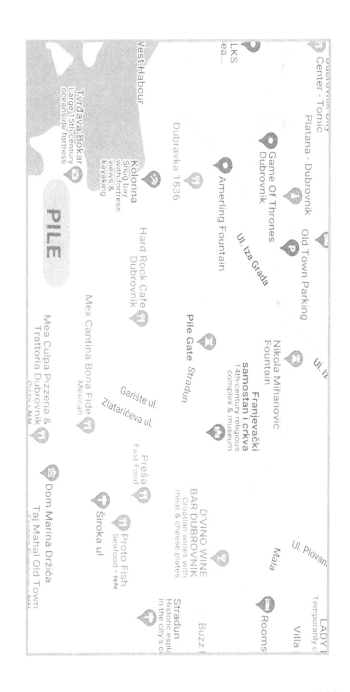

Dubrovnik City
Center - Tomic

Platana - Dubrovnik

Old Town Parking

Game Of Thrones
Dubrovnik

LKS
ea...

VestHabour

Tvrdava Bokar
Large 15th-century
oceanside fortress

Kolorina
Snug bay
with fortress
views &
kayaking

Dubravka 1836

Amerling Fountain

Ul. Iza Grada

PILE

Hard Rock Cafe
Dubrovnik

Mex Cantina Bona Fide
Mexican

Mea Culpa Pizzeria &
Trattoria Dubrovnik

Pile Gate   Stradun

Nikola Mihanović
Fountain

Franjevački
samostan i crkva
14th-century religious
complex & museum

Ul. Iz

Garište ul.

Zlatarićeva ul.

Preša
Fast Food

Proto Fish
Seafood · ₦₦

Dom Marina Držića

Taj Mahal Old Town

Široka ul

DVINO WINE
BAR DUBROVNIK
Croatian wines with
meat & cheese plates

Mala

Ul. Plovani

LADY I
Temporarily c

Villa

Rooms

Buzz I

Stradun
Historic espl.
in the city's c

116

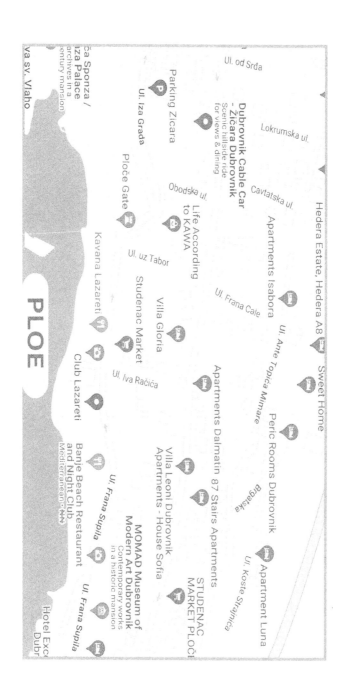

Ul. od Srda

ča Sponza /
iza Palace
archives in a
century mansion

va sv. Vlaho

Parking Zicara

Ul. iza Grada

Dubrovnik Cable Car
- Žičara Dubrovnik
Scenic hillside ride
for views & dining

Lokrumska ul.

Ploče Gate

Obodska ul.

Cavtatska ul.

Life According
to KAWA

Apartments Isabora

Hedera Estate, Hedera A8

Sweet Home

Kavana Lazareti

Ul. uz Tabor

Villa Gloria

Ul. Frana Cale

Ul. Ante Topića Mimare

PLOE

Studenac Market

Club Lazareti

Ul. Iva Račića

Apartments Dalmatin 87 Stairs Apartments

Peric Rooms Dubrovnik

Brgaška

Apartment Luna

Ul. Koste Strajnica

Banje Beach Restaurant
and Night Club
Mediterranean • $$

Ul. Frana Supila

Villa Leoni Dubrovnik
Apartments - House Sofia

STUDENAC
MARKET PLOČE

MOMAD Museum of
Modern Art Dubrovnik
Contemporary works
in a historic mansion

Ul. Frana Supila

Hotel Exc
Dubr

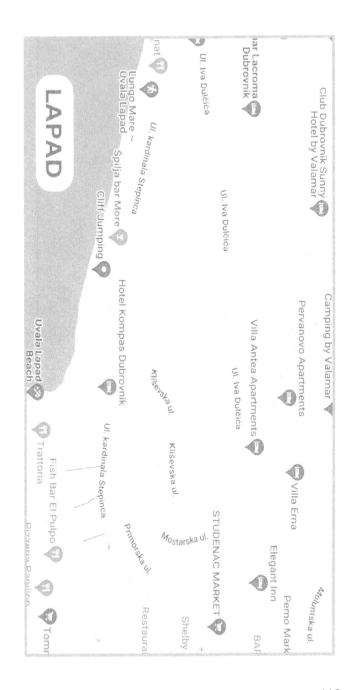

LAPAD

Club Dubrovnik Sunny
Hotel by Valamar

Bar Lacroma
Dubrovnik

Llungo Mare ~
Uvala Lapad

Ul. Iva Dulčića

Ul. kardinala Stepinca

Spilja bar More

Cliff Jumping

Uvala Lapad
Beach

Camping by Valamar

Pervanovo Apartments

Villa Antea Apartments

Ul. Iva Dulčića

Hotel Kompas Dubrovnik

Klíševska ul.

Ul. kardinala Stepinca

Klíševska ul.

Fish Bar El Pulpo

Trattoria

Villa Erna

Elegant Inn

STUDENAC MARKET

Mostarska ul.

Primorska ul.

Moluntska ul.

Perno Mark

BAF

Shelby

Restaura

Tomr

118

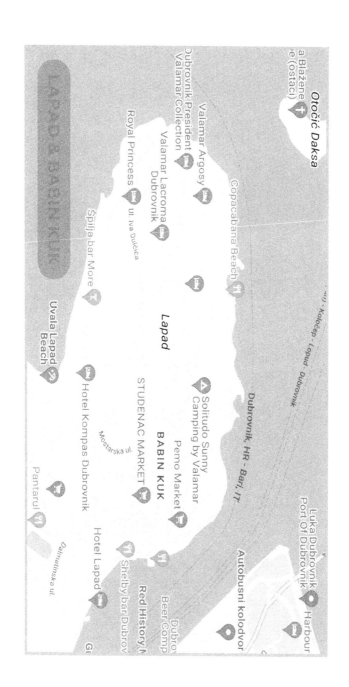

Otočić Daksa

a Blažene
e (ostaci)

Dubrovnik President
Valamar Collection

Valamar Argosy

Royal Princess

Valamar Lacroma
Dubrovnik

Copacabana Beach

Špilja bar More

ul. Iva Dulčića

LAPAD & BABIN KUK

Uvala Lapad
Beach

Lapad

Hotel Kompas Dubrovnik

Mostarska ul.

Pantarul

Dalmatinska ul.

Solitudo Sunny
Camping by Valamar

Pemo Market

STUDENAC MARKET

BABIN KUK

Dubrovnik, HR - Bari, IT

"IIJ - Koločep - Lopud - Dubrovnik"

Hotel Lapad

Shelby bar Dubrov

Red History N

Autobusni kolodvor

L.Luka Dubrovnik
Port Of Dubrovnik

Dubro
Beer Comp

Harbour

Gr

119

Printed in Great Britain
by Amazon

40664993R00066